EARTH'S CYCLES

The Plant Life Cycle

CHERYL JAKAB

Smart Apple Media

Smart Apple Media
2140 Howard Drive West
North Mankato, Minnesota 56003

First published in 2007 by
MACMILLAN EDUCATION AUSTRALIA PTY LTD
627 Chapel Street, South Yarra, Australia 3141

Visit our Web site at www.macmillan.com.au or go directly to www.macmillanlibrary.com.au

Associated companies and representatives throughout the world.

Copyright © Cheryl Jakab 2007

Library of Congress Cataloging-in-Publication Data

Jakab, Cheryl.
The plant life cycle / by Cheryl Jakab.
p. cm. — (Earth's cycles)
includes index.
ISBN 978-1-59920-147-4
1. Plant life cycles—Juvenile literature. I. Title.

QK49.J25 2007
580—dc22

2007004553

Edited by Erin Richards
Text and cover design by Christine Deering
Page layout by Christine Deering
Photo research by Jes Senbergs
Illustrations by Ann Likhovetsky, pp. 10, 12, 16, 17; Paul Könye, p. 29.

Printed in U.S.

Acknowledgements

The author and the publisher are grateful to the following for permission to reproduce copyright material:

Front cover photographs: seedling in soil cross-section (center), courtesy of Nature Production/Auscape; green foliage with yellow flowers (background), courtesy of Corbis.

Scott Bauer/Agricultural Research Service, p. 14; Jon Arnold Images / Alamy, p. 7; John T. Fowler/Alamy, p. 23 (top); Tim Gartside/Alamy, p. 15 (bottom); Holt Studios International Ltd/Alamy, p. 16; Michael van Ewijk/Auscape, p. 13 (right); Jean-Paul Ferrero/Auscape, p. 19 (bottom); Wayne Lawler/Auscape, p. 24; Nature Production/Auscape, p. 1, 11 (left); Jaime Plaza Van Roon/Auscape, p. 6; Steve Turner/Auscape, p. 23 (bottom); Corbis, pp. 4 (middle right & top left), 8, 20 (center & middle left); Getty Images, p. 19 (top); Andy Sacks/Getty Images, p. 9; David Sacks/Getty Images, p. 21 (top); iStockphoto.com, pp. 10, 18 (top), 22; Jiri Lochman/Lochman Transparencies, p. 28 (bottom); Marie Lochman/Lochman Transparencies, pp. 21 (bottom), 28 (top); Dennis Sarson/Lochman Transparencies, p. 26; Len Stewart/Lochman Transparencies, p. 17; NASA, p. 30; NPS Photo, p. 11 (right); Photodisc, pp. 4(bottom left, bottom right, middle left & top right), 15 (top), 18 (bottom), 20 (bottom left, bottom right, middle right & top), 25; Photolibrary, p. 5; Jaime Plaza/ Wildlight, p. 27; Trisha Sertori, p. 13 (left).

While every care has been taken to trace and acknowledge copyright, the publisher tenders their apologies for any accidental infringement where copyright has proved untraceable. Where the attempt has been unsuccessful, the publisher welcomes information that would redress the situation.

Contents

Seed

Young plant

Flower

Mature plant

ideas and tips

Glossary words
When a word is printed in **bold**, you can look up its meaning in the glossary on page 31.

Earth's natural cycles

What is a cycle?

A cycle is a never-ending series of changes that repeats again and again. Arrows in cycle diagrams show the direction in which the cycle is moving.

Earth's natural cycles create every environment on Earth. Living and non-living things are constantly changing. Each change is part of a natural cycle. Earth's natural cycles are working all the time.

Earth's non-living cycles are:
- the water cycle
- the rock cycle
- the seasons cycle

Earth's living cycles are:
- the food cycle
- the animal life cycle
- the plant life cycle

Seasons cycle

Food cycle

Water cycle

Plant life cycle

Animal life cycle

Rock cycle

Earth's natural cycles keep the planet healthy.

The balance of nature

Earth's natural cycles all connect with each other. The way the cycles connect is sometimes called the balance of nature.

Keeping the balance

Every living thing depends on Earth's natural cycles to survive. A change in one cycle can affect the whole balance of nature. Knowing how Earth's cycles work helps us keep the environment healthy.

Every living thing depends on the balance of nature to survive.

Plants

The plant kingdom is divided into two main groups, seed plants and non-seed plants. Seed plants include any plants that flower. Non-seed plants include ferns and mosses.

Plants are living things that produce their own food. They include mosses, ferns, grasses, herbs, bushes, vines, and trees. Plants can be so tiny that you need a microscope to see them. They can also be very big, such as tall redwood trees. There are more than 250,000 plant **species** on Earth. Plants are one of the five main kingdoms of living things. The other kingdoms are animals, fungi, bacteria, and single-celled life.

Plants are living things that make their own food.

6

The importance of plants

Plants are a very important part of the natural environment. Plants make up most of the living material on Earth.

Why are plants important to people?

People need plants to survive. Plants improve the quality of the air people breathe. They are used for food and for many other products. People enjoy plants in gardens, parks, and wilderness areas.

How do people affect plants?

People affect plants by cutting down forests and damaging natural **habitats**. These human activities have caused many plant species to become **endangered** or **extinct**.

How do plants fit into the balance of nature?

Plants are the base of most habitats on Earth. These include tropical rainforests, grasslands, and deserts. Plants hold soil together with their roots and are food for many animals.

The Amazon rainforest is home to many rare plant species.

The plant life cycle

The plant life cycle shows the different stages in the life of a plant. It shows how each plant starts life, grows up to become a **mature** plant and reproduces. There are more seed plants on Earth than non-seed plants. Most plants follow the life cycle of a seed plant.

Seed

Young plant

Mature plant

Flower

Plants move through different stages in the plant life cycle.

Different life cycles

Different plants have very different life cycles. How long it takes a plant to complete each stage depends on the species. The changes that occur at each stage of the cycle also vary depending on the species.

A walnut tree grows for many years before it becomes a mature plant.

Seed

Most plants begin life as a seed. A seed grows into the same type of plant that made the seed. Pumpkin seeds become pumpkin plants. Coconuts grow into coconut trees.

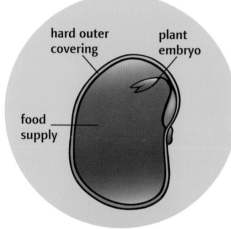

hard outer covering

plant embryo

food supply

Parts of a seed

Different parts of a seed carry out different functions. The hard outer covering of a seed protects the tiny plant **embryo** inside. Many seeds also contain a food supply for the embryo.

Dandelion seeds have wings and are carried to new places by the wind.

Seed growth

Seeds germinate, or sprout, when conditions are right. Water is needed to make a seed germinate. Many seeds can be stored in dry conditions for years, such as during a drought. They do not germinate until it has rained. The new plant, or seedling, uses food stored inside the seed to grow.

Some birds eat berries, and carry the seeds to new places in their droppings.

Many seeds germinate after it has rained.

11

Young plant

A seedling grows bigger to become a young plant in
the next stage of the plant life cycle. A young plant
grows if it gets enough food and water. After it has
used up the food in the seed, a young plant makes its
own food. Young plants grow very quickly.

Food for growing plants

Once a plant grows leaves and roots, it can make food
using sunlight and gases in the air. The roots of the
young plant take up water from the soil. The leaves take
in **carbon dioxide** from the air. The water and carbon
dioxide combine to make food for the plant. Sunlight
provides the energy for the plant to make its food.

Plants make their
own food using
energy from the sun.

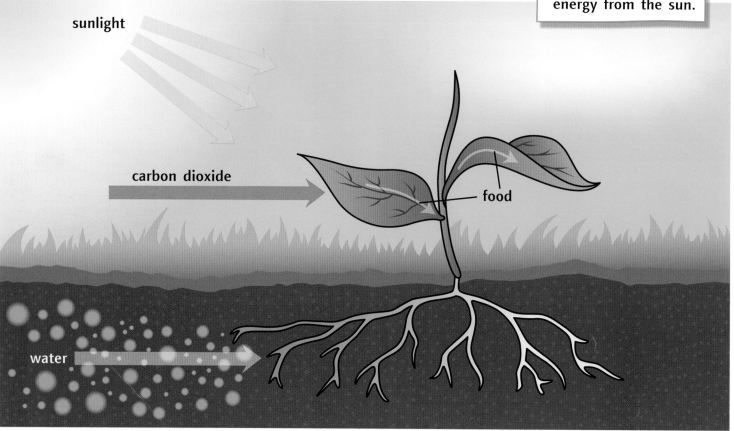

sunlight

carbon dioxide

food

water

12

Growth rate

Each young plant has its own growth rate. The growth rate is affected by how much water and **nutrients** the plant gets. The temperature of the air and soil also affects plant growth.

Parts of a young plant

Most plants have the same basic parts. These are:

- roots, which hold the plant in the soil and take up water and nutrients
- leaves, which produce food for the plant
- the trunk, branches, and stems, which are like a skeleton connecting all the parts

leaves

branches

roots

The roots of a mangrove tree are always above the ground.

Most forests have a combination of young and mature plants.

13

Mature plant

A young plant grows into a mature plant in the next stage of the plant life cycle. Different plants take different lengths of time to mature. Many plants are mature long before they grow to their largest size. Some plants, such as the sunflower, reach maturity in only a few weeks. Larger plants, including many trees, often grow for years before they reach maturity.

Sunflowers mature only weeks after the seeds germinate.

14

Mature plant growth

After they mature, plants continue to grow. Some grow slowly and others grow quickly. Many mature plants grow in a yearly cycle. **Deciduous trees** grow in areas where the winters are cold. They lose their leaves in fall to prepare for a period of slow growth during winter. New leaves appear in spring, and the trees do most of their growing in spring and summer.

Yearly growth cycles create rings in the trunks of deciduous trees.

The branches of deciduous trees are bare in winter.

15

Flower

Once a plant is fully mature, it can reproduce. This is what happens in the next stage of the plant life cycle. Most plants need flowers to reproduce. Some plants flower throughout the year, and others in certain seasons.

Reproduction

Flowers are the reproductive parts of most plants. Most flowers have both male and female parts. The female part produces **ova**. The male part produces **pollen**. Pollination takes place when male pollen joins with female ova. After time, the ovary swells and ripens into fruit. Inside the fruit, the ova develop into seeds.

Bees spread pollen as they move from flower to flower.

Helping pollination

Many flowers require pollen from a different flower to pollinate their ova. Wind and some animals help with pollination, by spreading pollen from flower to flower.

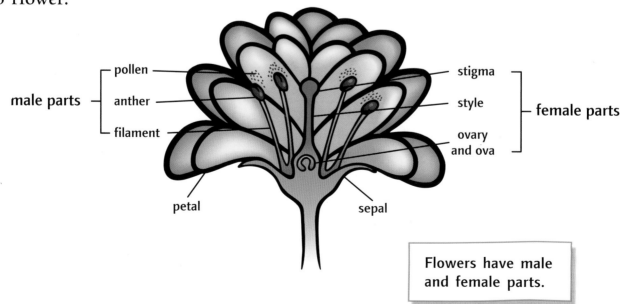

male parts — pollen — anther — filament

stigma — style — ovary and ova — female parts

petal   sepal

Flowers have male and female parts.

16

Reproduction without flowers

Some plants, such as ferns and mosses, reproduce with **spores** instead of flowers and seeds. Other plants reproduce **asexually**. Potatoes grow from tubers. Some plants can be grown from cuttings. Strawberry plants can reproduce by seeds or runners.

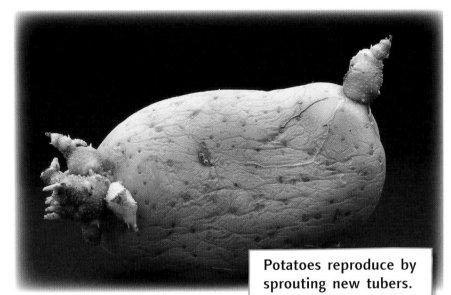

Potatoes reproduce by sprouting new tubers.

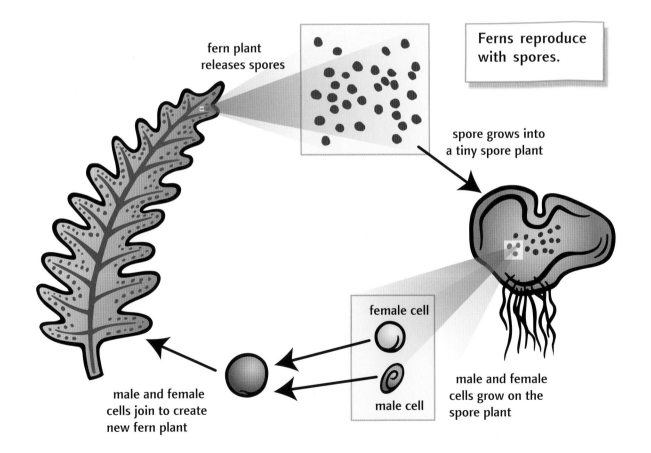

Ferns reproduce with spores.

fern plant releases spores

spore grows into a tiny spore plant

male and female cells grow on the spore plant

female cell

male cell

male and female cells join to create new fern plant

17

Plant life span

What is a plant life span?

Plants live and grow for a certain length of time and then die. This is called the life span of the plant. Each plant species has a different life span. Dying is also a part of the plant life cycle.

Different plant species have different life spans. Some live for only one year, some live for two years, and others live for many years.

Annuals

Plants with a life span of one year, such as sunflowers and tulips, are called annuals. An annual is a plant that goes through its whole life cycle and dies within a year.

Biennials

Plants with a life span of two years, such as parsley, are called biennials. During the first year, the young plant grows. In the second year, the plant produces flowers and seeds.

Biennials, such as parsley, complete their life cycle in two years.

Tulips are annuals, and only live for one year.

18

Perennials

Perennials live for a number of years. Some live for only a few years, while others live for much longer. Most perennials produce flowers and seeds many times during their life span.

The oldest living perennial

The creosote bush is believed to be the oldest living thing on Earth. Each bush grows for up to 100 years. The branches then split and bend over. The split branches develop their own roots in the soil and continue to grow. One creosote bush in the Mojave Desert in the United States has been splitting and growing for 11,700 years.

The creosote bush is the oldest living thing on Earth.

Death

Plants can die at any stage of the plant life cycle. A plant may be eaten by an animal, fall over or die of disease. A plant may die when young, after maturing, or live to a very old age. Many plants continue to live and grow as long as conditions are right.

The death of a tree provides food for fungi.

The balance of nature

The balance of nature shows how the plant life cycle is linked with Earth's other cycles. Plants have an effect on non-living and living things in every environment on Earth. The seasons, food, water, rocks, and animals all help to maintain the plant life cycle.

The plant life cycle is an important part of the balance of nature.

Plants and seasons

Many plant life cycles are linked to the seasons. In winter, plants often stop growing. In spring, many plants begin to bud and grow new leaves. Rising temperatures in the air and soil trigger the new plant growth.

Many trees grow new leaves in spring.

Plants, rocks, and soil

Most plants grow on the land with their roots anchored in the soil. They draw water and nutrients they need from the soil. Plant growth depends on the richness of the soil. The roots of plants also hold soil together.

Mangrove tree roots help hold the soil together.

Plants and water

Most plants need a regular supply of water to live and grow. Water from the soil is taken up through the roots of plants. Different plants require different amounts of water. Rainforest plants need a lot of water. Desert plants can survive with very little water.

A cactus can grow and survive in the desert where there is little water.

Plants and animals

Many plants depend on animals to pollinate them. Some animals also need plants to keep them alive. Baby caterpillars of the monarch butterfly feed only on milkweed plants. The butterfly must lay its eggs so the caterpillars hatch during the milkweed growing season.

The monarch butterfly must time its life cycle with that of the milkweed plant.

Plants and food

Plants produce the food in most habitats on Earth. Plants are a very important food source for most animals, including humans.

Plants are food for many animals, such as gorillas.

23

People and plants

People use plants in many different ways. This can affect the plant life cycle. Environmental weeds and land-clearing can endanger plant habitats.

Environmental weeds

When people take plants to places where they do not normally grow, they can become environmental weeds. Introduced species can reproduce very quickly and cover large areas of habitat. They compete with and take over **native** plants. Environmental weeds also threaten the animals that eat the native plants, since their natural food supply is removed.

This South American plant has become an environmental weed in both Australia and South Africa.

Land-clearing

People clear land for farming and for timber. Many areas that were once rich habitat are now cleared of plants. They no longer provide habitat for plants to live and grow. Plant cover all over Earth has been reduced, endangering many species. In 2002, more than 5,000 plant species were endangered. Many more plants that have not yet been discovered may also be endangered.

Large areas of forest all over Earth have been lost to farming.

25

Plant conservation

Plant conservation is the protection of plants on Earth. It includes protecting rare and endangered species to help them survive. Different methods of plant conservation include:

- protecting areas where rare and endangered species grow
- setting aside national parks and wilderness areas
- replanting cleared forests and grasslands
- collecting and germinating rare seeds
- tree planting projects to stop soil **erosion**

Planting trees can help stop erosion and produce richer soils for more plant growth.

26

The dinosaur tree

A tree named the Wollemi pine was around in the time of dinosaurs. Just like the dinosaurs, the Wollemi pine was thought to be extinct. In 1992, a wildlife officer named David Noble discovered a small group of living Wollemi pine trees. He found them growing in an isolated valley near Sydney, Australia.

Wollemi pine trees were around when dinosaurs were alive.

Saving the Wollemi pine

Research into the Wollemi pine has led to a clever protection plan. The trees grow well in pots and gardens, and are now sold as garden plants. The money raised from sales helps conserve Wollemi pines and other endangered plants and animals.

Protecting plants

Everyone can help protect plants. Getting active in your area, recycling, and reusing materials can help save plants.

Get active

- Grow vegetables in your garden
- Remove plants that could become environmental weeds
- Join tree planting projects in your local area

Recycle and reuse

- Keep plant scraps for compost
- Recycle paper to reduce the need to cut down trees
- Use plantation timber, not timber from old-growth forests

Growing rare plants in your garden stops them from becoming extinct.

Some plants, such as this lily from South Africa, can quickly become environmental weeds.

Growing plants

You can grow new plants yourself from seeds. You could choose to grow vegetables, garden flowers, or even a tree.

What you need
- plant pot
- water
- soil
- seeds

What to do

1 Fill the plant pot with soil and press it down firmly. Leave about 1 inch (2.5 cm) of space at the top of the pot.

2 Place the seeds on top of the soil. Cover them with a thin layer of soil.

3 Place the plant pot in a warm, sunny spot away from wind. Gently water the plant pot, being careful not to disturb the seeds.

4 Keep watering every couple of days. Label the plant pot with the name of the plant and the date the seeds were planted.

How long before the first seedlings appear?

Living with nature

We all depend on the balance of nature for our survival. If people continue to disturb Earth's cycles, it will upset the balance of nature. Understanding Earth's cycles helps us care for Earth and live in harmony with nature.

"The Earth does not belong to us: we belong to the Earth."

(Chief Seattle Suquamish leader, about 1854)

Glossary

asexually	without female and male parts
carbon dioxide	gas that plants take from the air as they live and grow
deciduous trees	trees that lose their leaves once a year
embryo	a new plant, developing inside a seed
endangered	in danger of dying out
erosion	the wearing away of rocks and soil
extinct	no longer existing
habitats	places where plants and animals naturally grow and live
mature	fully grown or developed
native	coming from or belonging to a certain place
nutrients	substances that give living things energy to live and grow
ova	female reproductive cells, egg cells
pollen	male reproductive cells of a flower
species	a particular type of animal or plant
spores	reproductive parts of ferns and mosses

Index